To _____

From _____

Other books by Exley:
Daughters ...   Sisters ...
True Love ...   For a Good Friend
Mothers ...   When Love is Forever
Missing You ...

Published simultaneously in 1996 by Exley Publications in Great
Britain and Exley Giftbooks in the USA.

12 11 10 9 8 7 6 5 4 3

Border illustrations by Juliette Clarke
Copyright © Helen Exley 1996
The moral right of the author has been asserted.

ISBN 1-85015-709-X

Edited and pictures selected by Helen Exley.
Picture research by Image Select International.
Typeset by Delta, Watford.
Printed and bound in China.

Exley Publications Ltd, 16 Chalk Hill, Watford, Herts. WD1 4BN, UK.
Exley Publications LLC, 232 Madison Avenue, Suite 1206, NY 10016, USA.

To my Husband ~ with Love

QUOTATIONS SELECTED BY
*H*ELEN EXLEY

EXLEY
NEW YORK • WATFORD, UK

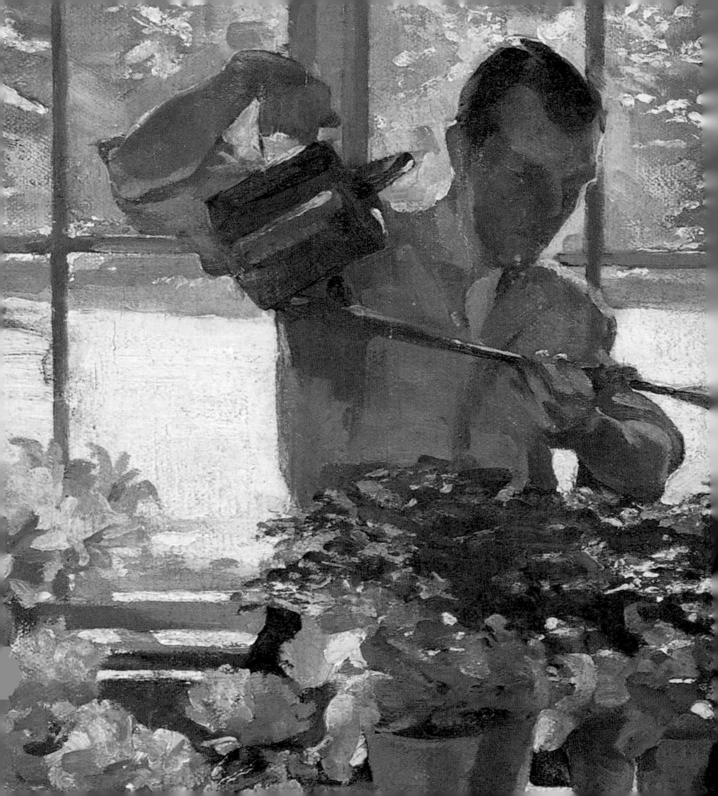

Constant in a world of change, understanding in a world of indifference, loving and passionate in a world that often hates. He is the sharing of joy and sorrow, the end of loneliness, my lover and the father of my children.

MARION MARSHALL

A husband is someone who forgets your birthday, forgets your anniversary, but also forgets your grey hairs and wrinkles.

BETTY MORRIS

He is the one who sits patiently holding his hands in front of him pretending to be a pelvis whilst you endlessly practise delivering a breech teddy-bear!

SUSAN SHUFFLEBOTTOM

Sexiness wears thin after a while and beauty fades, but to be married to a man who makes you laugh every day, ah, now that's a real treat!

JOANNE WOODWARD

He's the typical "no-nonsense", mustn't show his feelings, man, who wept when you refused his first proposal of marriage.

JENNY CLEMENTS

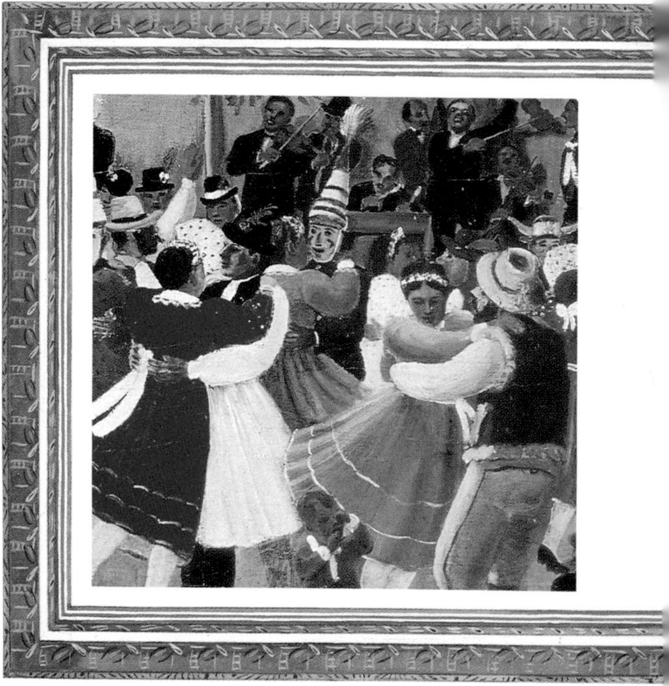

I look back to the early days of our acquaintance and friendship as to the days of love and innocence, and, with an indescribable pleasure, I have seen near a score of years roll over our heads with an affection heightened and improved by time, nor have the dreary years of absence in the smallest degree effaced from my mind the image of the dear untitled man to whom I gave my heart.

ABIGAIL ADAMS TO JOHN ADAMS,
FUTURE PRESIDENT OF THE UNITED STATES

Over the years,
When the sink overflowed
Or the car ran out of gas
Or the lady who comes every Tuesday to clean
didn't come
Or I felt pudgy. Or misunderstood
Or inferior to Marilyn Kaufman who is not only a
pediatric surgeon but also a very fine person as well
as beautiful
Or I fell in the creek and got soaked on our first family
camping trip
Or mosquitoes ate me alive on our first family
camping trip
Or I walked through a patch of what later turned
out to be plenty of poison ivy on what later turned
out to be our last family camping trip
Or my sweater shrank in the wash
Or I stepped on my glasses
Or the keys that I swear on my children's head I put
on the top of the dresser weren't there
Or I felt depressed. Or unfulfilled
Or inferior to Ellen Jane Garver who not only teaches

constitutional law but is also a wit plus sexually insatiable
Or they lost our luggage
Or our reservations
Or two of the engines
Or the rinse that was going to give my hair some
subtle copper highlights turned it purple
Or my mother-in-law got insulted at
something I said
Or my stomach got upset at something I ate
Or I backed into a truck that I swear when I looked
in my rear-view mirror wasn't parked there
Or I suffered from some other blow of fate,
It's always been so nice to have my husband by my
side so I could
Blame him.

JUDITH VIORST, FROM "AMONG OTHER
THOUGHTS ON OUR WEDDING ANNIVERSARY"

Some say a husband can't be changed. Untrue. Both partners change in an equal marriage, and he's the man who you finally reach the finishing line with, because he's there beside you, not in front of or behind you.

GILLIAN D.S. WARNER

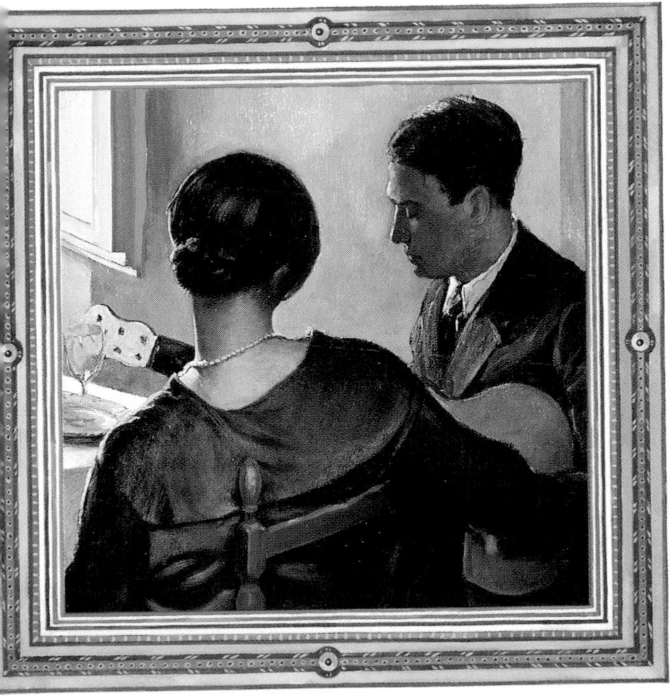

A HUSBAND IS ...

... the man asleep in front of the television on Sunday afternoons.

... the man ten steps behind when you want to look at underwear.

... the man ten steps ahead when he wants to look at cameras.

... the man standing staring wistfully at sports cars in showroom windows.

... the man doing sums on the backs of envelopes.

… the man kicking the mower.

… the man who finds it difficult to admit anything
is entirely his own fault.

… the man who says you're looking much, much
better this morning, when you're in the
second day of 'flu.
(The washing is piling up.)

… the man whose eyes deteriorate just in time
to not be able to see the bags and sags and wrinkles
and blotches and such.

PAM BROWN, b.1928

The joys of marriage?

Solemn things. Silly things.

Your hand to take mine in times of trouble. In times of joy.

The sound of your key in the lock;

of your quiet breathing in the darkness.

The smell of your shaving cream.

And things — tokens of your presence.

Your book, left open on the bedside table.

Your ancient gardening jacket hung behind the kitchen door.

The sight of you, a shadow among shadows, out in the garden,

making the most of the last of the light.

PAM BROWN, b.1928

An enormous part of my past does not exist
without my husband. An enormous part of
my present, too. I still feel somehow that
things do not really happen to me unless I
have told them to him.

ANNA QUINDLEN

Whenever I go out of the village
and see a stone
or a tree in the distance,
I think:
It is my husband.

SONG OF A WOMAN WHOSE HUSBAND HAD GONE
TO THE COAST TO EARN MONEY

Without you, dearest dearest I couldn't see or hear or feel or think – or live – I love you so and I'm never in all our lives going to let us be apart another night. It's like begging for mercy of a storm or killing Beauty or growing old, without you. I want to kiss you so – and in the back where your dear hair starts and your chest – I love you – and I can't tell you how much – To think that I'll *die* without your knowing – Goofo, you've *got* to try [to] feel how much I do – how inanimate I am when you're gone.

ZELDA FITZGERALD (1900-1948),
TO F. SCOTT FITZGERALD

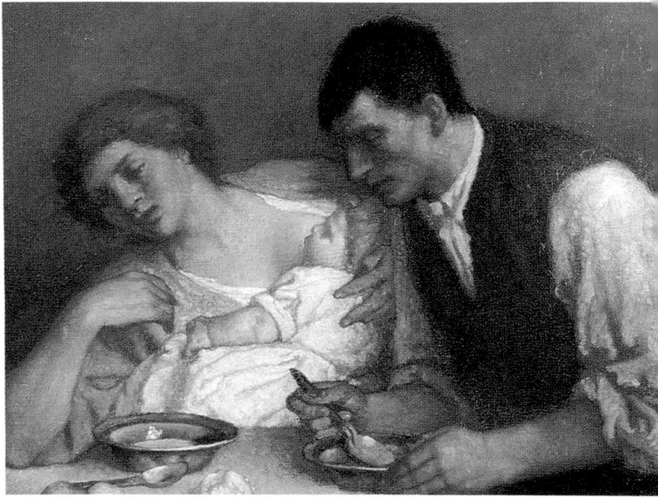

How very new you were. How could I have known, or guessed, what you'd become? I loved you dearly – but you, I see now, were half unmade. And, surely, that is the joy of marriage – to see Time shape the stone, to watch it carve the man. I look at your dear face, your hands, and know each stroke that made them as they are. I love each line, each altered plane. How good it's been to share these years with you.

CHARLOTTE GRAY, b.1937

Coming across the word "infanticide" in my newspaper, I commented to my wife, who was knitting and trying to follow a pattern, on the different words used to denote various types of murder – homicide, fratricide, matricide, and so on. I then asked her, "Is there a special word used when a wife murders her husband?"
Without missing a stitch she retorted: "Pesticide."

JOHN HUGHES

As her husband advanced up the path she had a sudden vision of their three years together. Those years were her whole life; everything before them had been colorless and unconscious, like the blind life of the plant before it reaches the surface of the soil. The years had not been exactly what she had dreamed; but if they had taken away certain illusions they had left richer realities in their stead. She understood now that she had gradually adjusted herself to the new image of her husband as he was, as he would always be. He was not the hero of her dreams, but he was the man she loved, and who had loved her. For she saw now, in this last wide flash of pity and initiation, that, as a comely marble may be made out of worthless scraps of mortar, glass, and pebbles, so out of mean mixed substances may be fashioned a love that will bear the stress of life.

EDITH WHARTON (C.1861-1937).
FROM "TALES OF MEN AND GHOSTS"

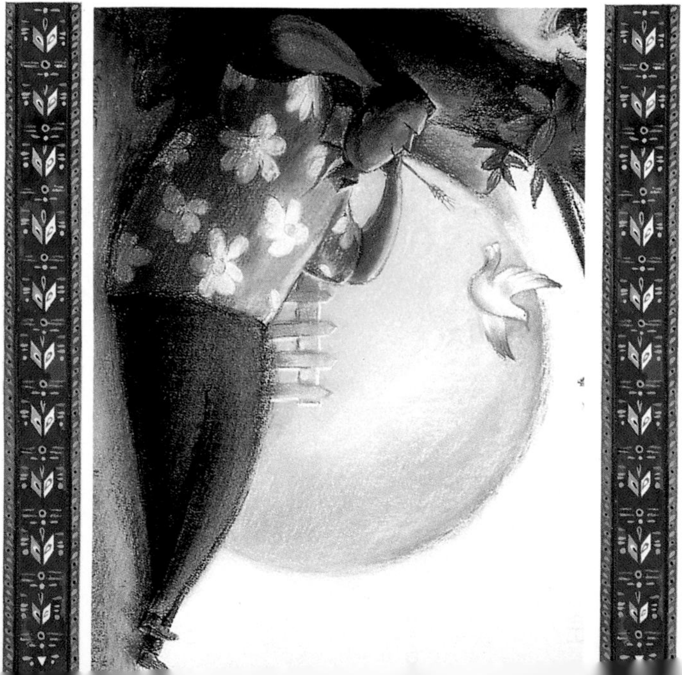

He provides honourable excuses for doing nothing when
household mechanisms are doing likewise.

J. S. BARBER

efore marriage, a man declares that he would lay down his life
to serve you; after marriage, he won't even lay down his
newspaper to talk to you.

HELEN ROWLAND (1876-1905),
FROM "A GUIDE TO MEN"

The best way to get most husbands to do something is to
suggest that perhaps they're too old to do it!

ANNE BANCROFT

… it is utterly impossible that I should ever forget this – that I should ever forget that you were once my lover and are my husband and the father of my children. I cannot behold you without emotion; my heart still answers to your voice, my blood in my veins to your footsteps.

FANNY KEMBLE (1809-1893)

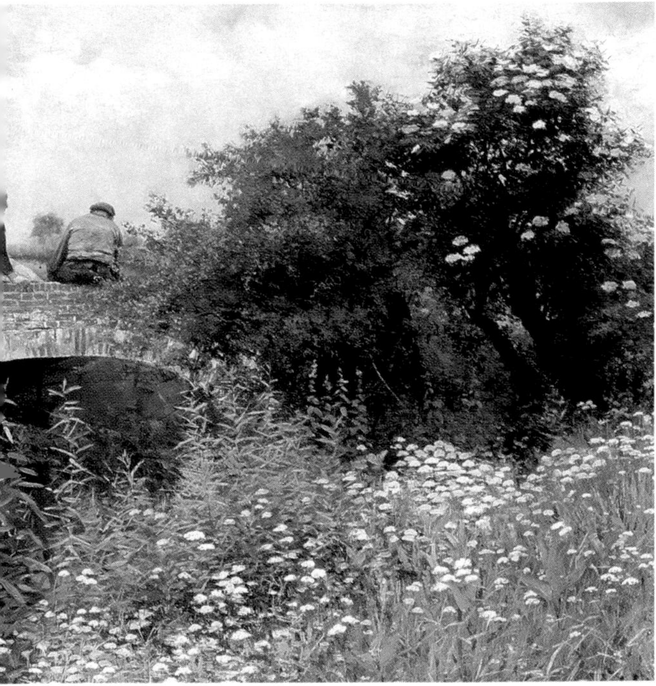

Sometimes when he saw how happy I was
he would say:
"Helen, you ought to have a different sort of husban
one who would always be happy and careless and
never cruel, who would always love your untidiness
I love it now, and not mind your short sight as I don
mind it now, and kiss you much oftener as I kiss you
now." "Well then" I would say, "perhaps if you
were such a husband, I should be somebody
different too, and perhaps not so happy as
I certainly am now. So that's that."

HELEN THOMAS, FROM "UNDER STORM'S WING"

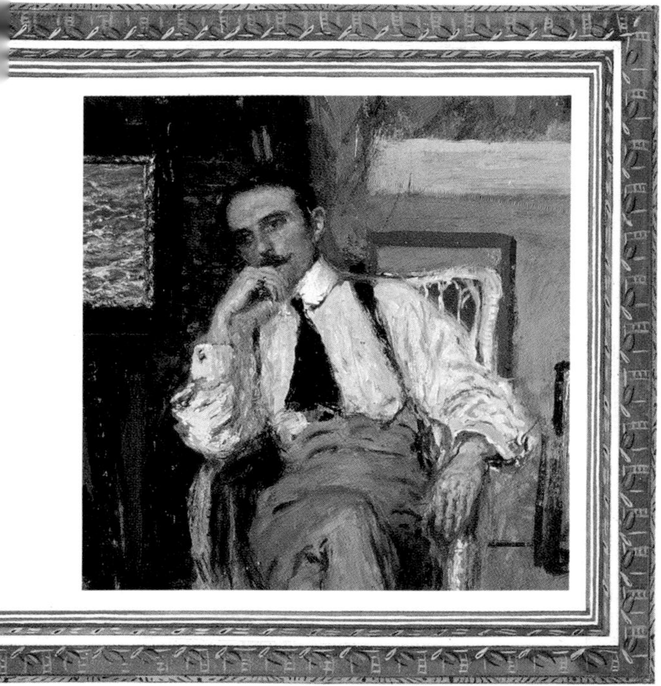

No woman was ever nearer to her mate than I am – ever more absolutely bone of his bone, and flesh of his flesh. I know no weariness of my Edward's society – he knows none of mine, any more than we each do of the pulsation of the heart that beats in our separate bosoms; consequently, we are ever together. To be together is for us to be at once as free as in solitude, as gay as in company.

CHARLOTTE BRONTE (1816-1855),
FROM "JANE EYRE"

It is a lovely thing to have a husband and a wife

developing together and having the feeling of falling in

love again. That is what marriage really means.

Helping one another to reach the full status of being

persons, responsible and autonomous beings who do no

run away from life.

PAUL TOURNIER (1898-1986)

... I have friends, I have thousands of friendly acquaintances; there are people that I like and people that I dislike: but standing apart there is only him.

CATHERINE COOKSON, b.1906,
FROM "LET ME MAKE MYSELF PLAIN"

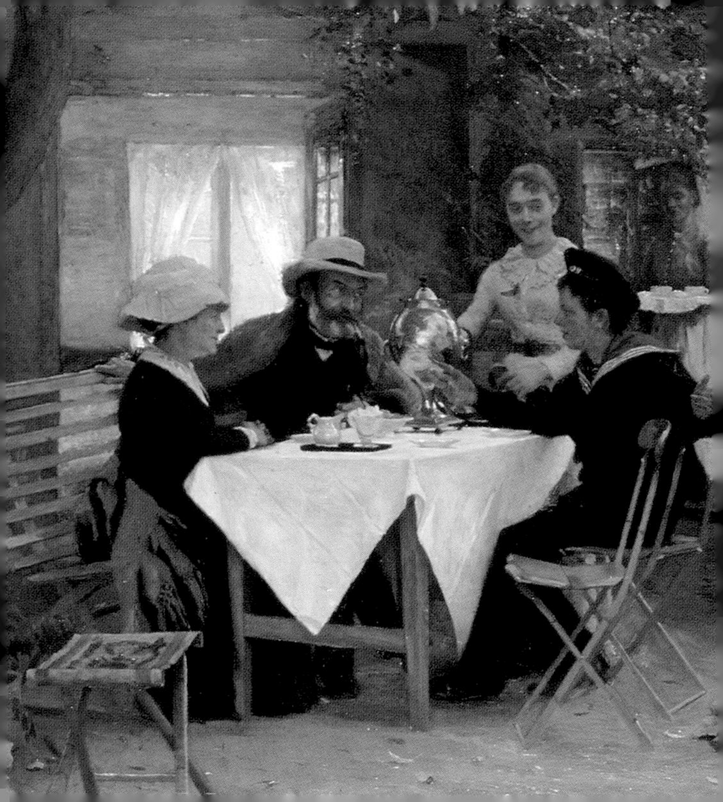

How proud I was to say "My husband...." – A
grown woman and yet feeling suspiciously like a
child playing a game. Signing my new name.
Trying to look long-married.
And did you feel the same? Turning the key in
the lock. Sharing the news of the day. Talking
tax and mortgages.
We look back now on those dear amateurs –
blundering to understand, learning to be
married. And we are still learning – though
with more confidence than when we first began.
Marriage is a voyage of discovery
that takes a lifetime!

PAM BROWN, b.1928

After you have worn a dress for about two years, a husband will say 'That's nice, dear, is it new?'

ELIZABETH SIMMS

Yes, I love him. I love those hick shirts he wears with those boiled cuffs and the way he always has his vest buttoned wrong. He looks like a giraffe, and I love him. I love him because he's the kind of a guy who gets drunk on a glass of buttermilk, and I love the way he blushes right up to his ears. I love him because he doesn't know how to kiss – the jerk! I love him Joe.

CHARLES BRACKETT, BILLY WILDER,
FROM "BALL OF FIRE", 1941

He's a chump, you know. That's what I love about
him. That and the way his ears wiggle when he gets
excited. Chumps always make the best husbands.
When you marry, Sally, grab a chump. Tap his
forehead first, and if it rings solid, don't hesitate.
All the unhappy marriages come from the
husband having brains.
What good are brains to a man?
They only unsettle him.

P. G. WODEHOUSE (1881-1975),
FROM "THE ADVENTURES OF SALLY"

A husband is someone who phones you up from
the office to ask you the number of his car (parked
outside the office) and then says "Thanks, son!"

PATRICIA STRANG

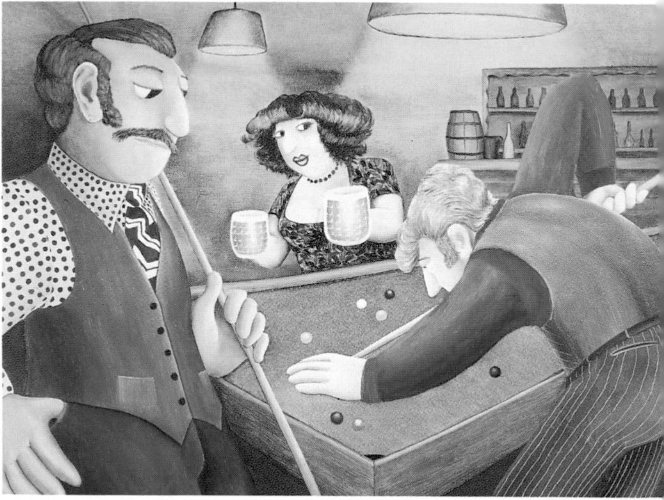

There you are you see, quite simply, if you cannot

have your dear husband for a comfort and a

delight, for a breadwinner and a crosspatch, for a

sofa, a chair or a hotwater bottle, one can use

him as a Cross to be borne.

STEVIE SMITH (1902-1971)

Don't leave me, beloved, on this plane
Without your hand to grasp in the night
And your voice to wake me from sleep
And your love to wrap my day in kindness,
Fold on fold,
And tell me that I'm young,
And that age
Could never make me old.

CATHERINE COOKSON, b.1906,
FROM "LET ME MAKE MYSELF PLAIN"

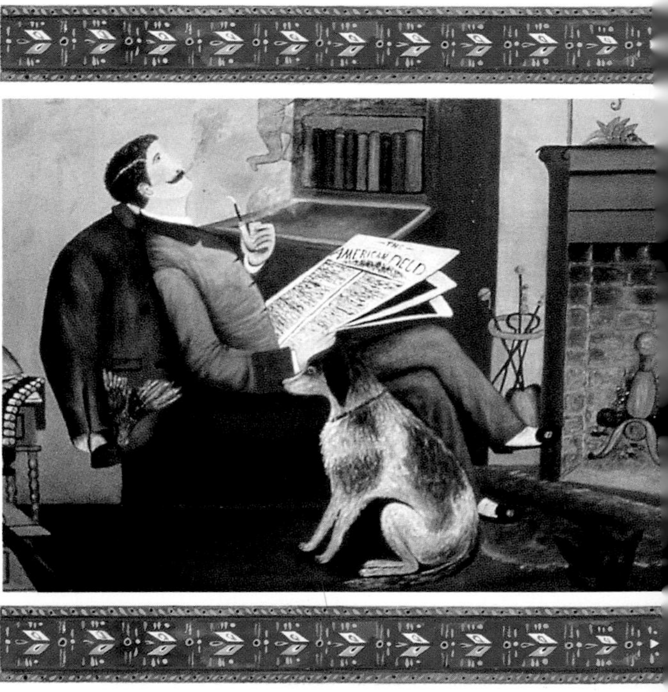

"Don't ye know what this is?" says she.

"Sure," says he, "it's Choosdah."

"No, but what day?"

"I give it up. St Pathrick's day, Valentine's day,
pay day. What's th' answer?"

"But think."

"I give it up."

"It's th' annyvarary iv our weddin'."

"Oh," says he, "so it is. I'd clean f'rgot. That's right.
I raymimber it well, now that ye mintion it.
Well, betther luck nex' time."

FINLEY PETER DUNNE

*I*t seems to me, to myself, that no man was ever before to any woman what you are to me – the fulness must be in proportion, you know to the vacancy ... and only I know what was behind – the long wilderness without the blossoming rose ... and the capacity for happiness, like a black gaping hole, before this silver flooding.

ELIZABETH BARRETT BROWNING (1806-1861),
TO ROBERT BROWNING

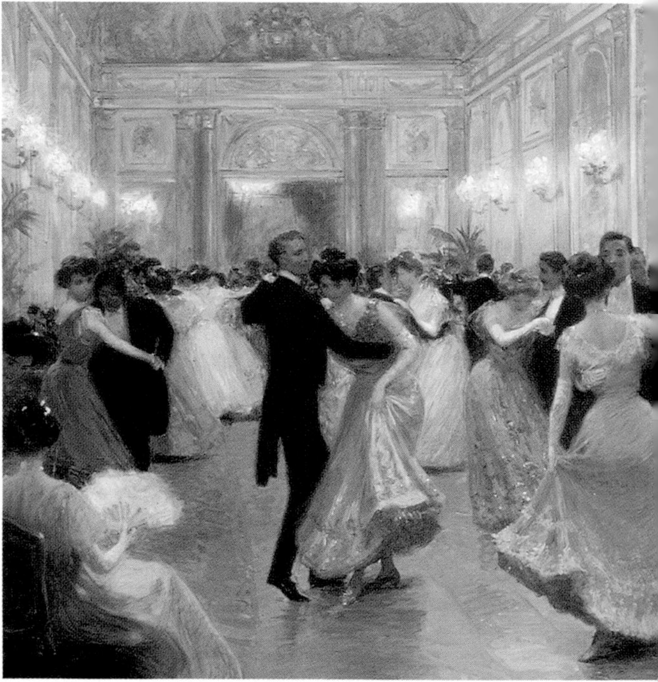

Loved and respected by a husband I love and respect, my duties and my pleasures are combined. I am happy, and I ought to be. If there exist more acute pleasures I do not want to know them. Is there a sweeter pleasure than to be at peace with oneself?... What you call happiness is but a turmoil of the senses, a tempest of passions which it is frightening to witness even from the safety of the shore....

CHODERLOS DE LACLOS
(1741-1803),
FROM "LES LIAISONS
DANGEREUSES"

I watch from the window – see you among the bean rows, a shadow among shadows. I lay the table, peer into the oven, call you from the kitchen door. You look toward me, wave. The bats flicker above your head. An owl screeches somewhere beyond the trees. And I am happy – held in this quietness, this certainty. For this is love – we two, bound together by time and shared experience. Easy with one another. Linked by habit and affection. A lifetime's memories. Eternal love.

CHARLOTTE GRAY, b.1937

Dear husbands. Dear companions.
Dear friends.
What do we ask of you? A few things.
A thousand things. Great and small. Solemn and
utterly superficial. We ask you to respect us, trust
us, share with us. We ask you to put your grubby
clothes in the laundry basket, to put the cap back
on the toothpaste, to leave your gardening boots
at the kitchen door.
We learn about one another little by little, year
by year – filing away preferences and habits and
the things that trigger temper – or delight. We
grapple with differences of taste and opinion,
with irritations, aggravations, and what at times
seems very like pig-headedness. We discover each
other's deeply-rooted oddities. And weaknesses.
And fears. Little by little, year by year, we grow
accustomed to each other, until even the

exasperations assume a comfortable familiarity.
Though some will prickle, like a tiny thorn in a
shoe, all our lives long.
And none of it works without love. With love,
difficulties are simply to be faced and dealt with.
Lacking love, they are twigs, branches, tree
trunks, added to a destructive fire.
With love this is the very best of all
relationships. Through it we grow wiser, more
tolerant, perceptive, kind. Through it we learn to
be human and adult.
So, what do I ask of you?
Just to be there. The vital part of my existence.

PAM BROWN, b.1928

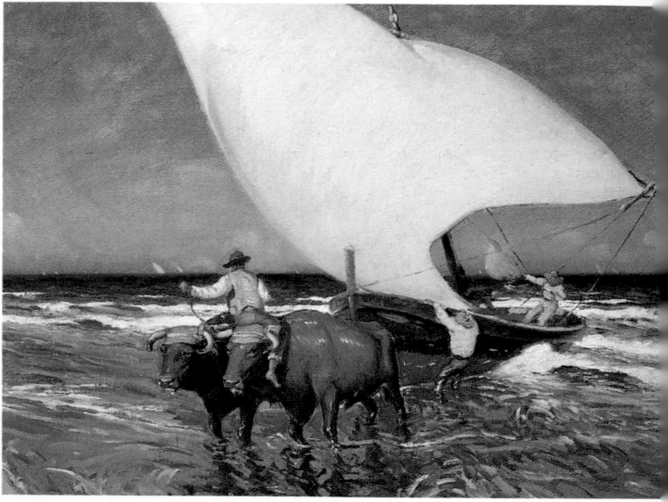

*To be loved and chosen by a good man is the best and
sweetest thing which can happen to a woman.*

LOUISA MAY ALCOTT (1832-1888),
FROM "LITTLE WOMEN"

*I've been given every bit of support that any woman
would ever want. He has always been there for me.
He is a great rock.*

CONNIE CHUNG,
ON HER HUSBAND, MAURY POVICH

A good husband makes a good wife.

ROBERT BURTON (1577-1640)

I have now been married ten years. I know
what it is to live entirely for and with what I
love best on earth. I hold myself supremely
blest – blest beyond what language can
express because I am my husband's life as fully
as he is mine.

CHARLOTTE BRONTE (1816-1855),
FROM "JANE EYRE"

For one man is my world of all the men

This wide world holds; O love, my world is you.

CHRISTINA ROSSETTI (1830-1874)

I bless you.

I kiss and caress every tenderly beloved place

and gaze into your deep, sweet eyes which

long ago conquered me completely.

Love ever grows.

TSARITSA ALEXANDER TO TSAR
NICHOLAS II OF RUSSIA (1868-1918)

Two people holding each other up

like flying buttresses. Two people

depending on each other and babying

each other and defending each other

against the world outside. Sometimes it

was worth all the disadvantages of

marriage just to have that: one friend

in an indifferent world.

ERICA JONG, b.1942,
FROM "FEAR OF FLYING"

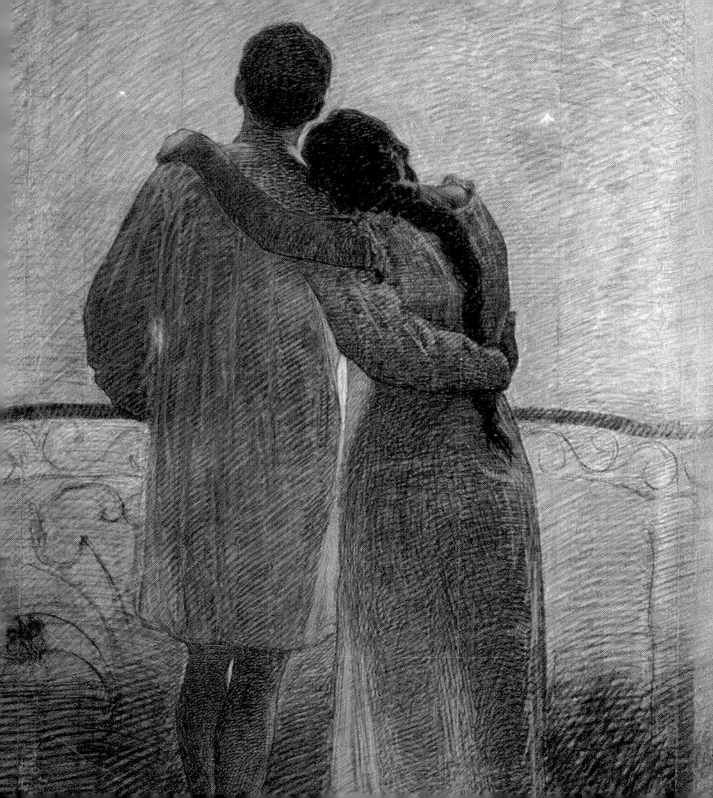

Acknowledgements: The publishers are grateful for permission to reproduce copyright material. While every effort has been made to trace copyright holders, the publishers would be pleased to hear from any not here acknowledged. CATHERINE COOKSON: extracts from "Let Me Make Myself Plain", published by Bantam, a division of Transworld Publishers, 1988. All rights reserved. Also reprinted with permission of Sheil Land Associates; ZELDA FITZGERALD: extract from "Zelda Fitzgerald" by Nancy Milford © 1970 Nancy Milford. Reprinted by permission of Laurence Pollinger Ltd. on behalf of The Estate Of Zelda Fitzgerald and Harold Ober Associates Inc.; MARGARET LANE: extract from "Letter To My Daughter" published in The Reader's Digest, June 1976; HELEN THOMAS: extract from "Under Storm's Wing" published by Grafton Books, a division of HarperCollins Publishers Ltd. 1990; JUDITH VIORST: "Among Other Thoughts On Our Wedding Anniversary" taken from "How Did I Get To Be 40 And Other Atrocities" by Judith Viorst © 1973, 1974, 1976 by Judith Viorst, published by Simon & Schuster; EDITH WHARTON: extract from "Tales Of Men And Ghosts".

Picture Credits: Exley Publications is very grateful to the following individuals and organizations for permission to reproduce their pictures: Alinari (ALI), Bonhams, London (BON), The Bridgeman Art Library (BAL), Edimedia (EDM),